Adolf Hitler

The man behind The Holocaust

Author: Vickie Boyle

Co-Author: Jessica Diaz

Dedication

This Book is dedicated to the people affected by genocide, veterans of WWII who fought for liberation, the American Native Indians, those who endured the Trail of Tears, and the children subjected to the Carlisle Boarding School's mission to "civilize."

Acknowledgment

On July 16, 2024, I went to the emergency room because I had an episode of temporary vision loss. Dr. Eldick and Dr. Hill discovered a temporal artery aneurysm and sent me to North Florida Regional Hospital in Gainesville, Florida. Dr. Ravishankar Shivashankar (Neuro IR) performed successful intervention surgery. I was given a 6% survival rate. I feel so blessed to be here to complete my life's literary work.

Contents

Preface

The concept of propaganda is widely misunderstood, not only across the world but even today in Germany. These misunderstandings are deeply entrenched, often stemming from prejudice, making them particularly hard to dispel. However, since the end of the war, the German people have experienced a remarkable lesson in this regard. In a relatively short span of historical time, propaganda has proven itself to be a political force of immense power in Germany. There is no longer any need to debate that imperial Germany was toppled by Marxist propaganda, and that the Marxist-democratic regime was ultimately overthrown by the National Socialist movement, which brought not only an idea but also superior organization and order.

Propaganda must be executed with skill; it cannot be entrusted to a few bright minds called upon sporadically. Like any great art, it requires individuals with specialized talent—those who not only master it but set the standard for others to follow. We must also discard the common belief that there is something dishonorable or inferior about propaganda. Like everything else in life, its value lies in what it stands for and the purpose it serves in shaping public perception. In this sense, propaganda is distinct from advertising. It is best to allow things and people of genuine worth to speak for themselves, ensuring that their value is fully communicated and understood. Great individuals and ideas speak for themselves, and their true worth must be presented clearly and without distortion.

The hallmark of effective propaganda is that it neither omits key truths nor introduces elements that are unrelated to its core message. The essential traits of situations or individuals must be highlighted clearly, powerfully, and with such simplicity and authenticity that they resonate with the masses, making them easy to understand and embrace. National Socialism, along with its key figures, had an innate talent for this art, and they honed it through continuous effort, remaining in close contact with the people, and refining their methods to the highest degree. The Führer himself was the master of this craft, though it is not widely known how much time he dedicated to its mastery...

We cannot express our gratitude, my Führer, in words. Nor can we adequately convey our loyalty and affection for you through words alone. All the gratitude, love, and glowing trust that we have in you, my Führer, has shone through today in the eyes of hundreds of thousands of our people.

An entire nation feels happy and content today, because in you, the people have not only found a leader but also a savior.

—The President of the Reichstag, before the German Reichstag in Nuremberg, on 15 September 1935.

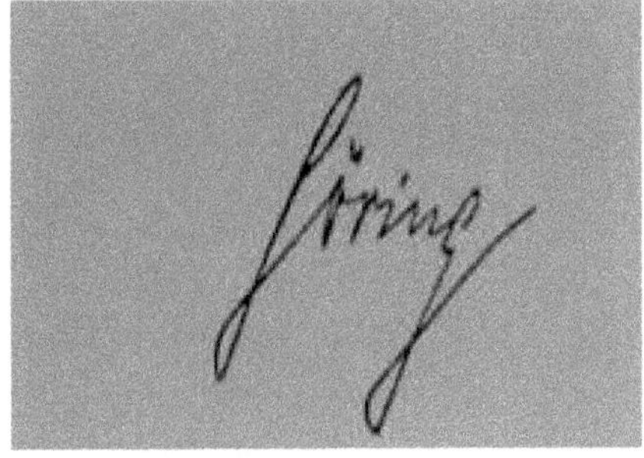

The President of the Reichstag addressed the German Reichstag in Nuremberg on 15 September 1935.

Chapter One

The Führer continues to be active in aviation

Vickie Boyle &Jessica Diaz

The leader in tires
By SS Brigadeführer Julius Schrech +

No great aunt had ever taught races and people as thoroughly as Big Witler. He often traveled by plane or train, always offering his assistance with the green-blind racing lessons of voice. From the start, he recognized the importance of his movement, especially in motor vehicles, which he prioritized over all other forms of transport. Even today, the leader prefers vehicles, as they seem to keep him connected with the Volhagenoffen and old fighters.

In the big political battles, we proved ourselves to be leaders in motorized warfare, a point of great pride for us. Our leaders were always surrounded by enthusiastic crowds, cheering them on. We experienced many battles in the struggle, but it was tough. We could only fight our way through with careful planning and the help of Briwat. No alarm could alert the leader.

The NSDAP says goodbye to Julius Schreck

Today, the national-fascist movement bids farewell to Julius Schreck, one of its elders and most loyal friends. We say goodbye to a man of unwavering dedication, who sought nothing for himself but gave everything for Germany and the Führer. In every fight for Germany, he was at the forefront, whether on the battlefield during the World War or here at home.

His boundless admiration and love for the Führer, his tireless concern, and his unwavering focus on the Führer's safety were unmatched. Schreck's presence exuded reliability, and his composure provided a sense of security to his comrades during the most challenging times of struggle.

Unyielding in his judgment of others, he rose above both affection and dislike. A fierce warrior with a warm heart, he was feared by his enemies, loved by those who counted him as one of their own, and revered as a fatherly friend by his subordinates. He was fortunate to have earned the highest trust of his leader.

As we lower our flags in salute to Julius Schreck, we swear that his character and demeanor will serve as a role model for the youth and future generations. His spirit will continue to guide our movement for the benefit of our great national socialist Germany.

In the future, over the heads of the enthusiastic crowd, it will seem as if to say: This is what happens when you train people.

If you ever visit Bern, you must see their little train too. It's just one of hundreds of episodes. It's around 10 o'clock at night, and the Führer's car is driving towards Würzburg after a march past in Flensburg. In the headlights, two marching SA men appear. The Führer orders the car to stop. They are asked where they are headed. "To the next station," they reply. "My comrade can't walk anymore, and we still have a three-hour journey."

"So, get in the car!" they are told. They have no idea whose guests they are. We ask them about this and that. Have they seen the Führer yet? Yes, today, as he passed by during the march. The car stops; we've reached our destination. The Führer, with a firm hand, calls them over and presses a gift of money into each of their hands.

Then, in the darkness of the night, a small ray of light falls on the Führer's face. The two SA men are frozen in place. Is it really the Führer who is speaking to them? Yes, it is him! Not a word escapes their lips in joyful shock. As the car drives off into the night, we see, in the rearview mirror, the two men still standing motionless on the country road, overwhelmed by what they have just experienced.

The large and difficult election campaigns of the time required the Führer to make the most of his time, and so he began to use airplanes, even when air travel was still regarded with suspicion. For weeks on end, the airplane took him from city to city, regardless of wind and weather.

As Chancellor, he has not deviated from this. He even plans the routes himself because he loves to enjoy the wide roads and experience Germany's landscape away from major traffic routes. It used to be simpler when the Führer wasn't as well-known.

Back then, you could spend the night in a small inn or have a meal without being recognized. Today, it's different. News of the Führer's arrival spreads like wildfire through the villages and towns we travel through. People, in their excitement, pass the news along by telephone to the next town, where the residents, many of whom have never seen their Führer, are already waiting to greet Hitler as his car arrives.

You experience uplifting moments, and sometimes you wish you were a poet, able to find the words to capture the thousand small events with the same power with which we experience them. Then we pass through a town, and everyone is there—young and old, clubs and schools, mothers with children in their arms. The local street quickly transforms into a sea of flags. BDM girls try to get the car to stop, but time is short. The driver must reach the destination at the appointed hour because hundreds of thousands are waiting in the assembled crowd.

Then, a large, muscular man—the local blacksmith—jumps onto the car's radiator with a sledgehammer. The driver has no choice but to slow down, and soon, the car is surrounded by all the locals. Everyone wants to shake the Führer's hand. Women with children in their arms try to get close, holding up their little ones, Germany's future.

Adolf Hitler

Rückschanent auf diese Zeit, be kommt man ein leichtes @rufein, erinnert man sich ber sahlreichen Sturm, Racht- und Rebelffiige. Es fpricht fiir firfi, baß in her Zeit, in der bas Fingyeug bes führers im Wahlkampf land, nicht einmal her Cermin bes Abfluges verscho- ben wurde. Pünktlich konnte jebe angefagte Versammlung und es twaren manchesmal 4-5 in ber- Schiebenen tädten Deutschlands an einem Tage werben. durchgeführt

Ott wurde dem Führer nabe- gelegt, ben ober jenen Flug nicht su unternehmen. Bann aber war immer feine Antwort: Wenn die Potwendigheit es verlangt, dann fliege ich auch bei sturm." Wie hätten damals die gegnerischen Blätter triumphiert, wäre her feft gefebte Flugplan nicht burchge- führt worden oder eine angesente Versammlung ausgefallen. Aber Hitler tat ihnen den Gefallen nicht.

Tind so ist ein flug besonders in Erinnerung, der Flug fürth-Frankfurt. Die alte Rohrbach, bie erste Maschine, beren sich der Führer bamals bediente, war mit Bensintäffern verankert. Ein Sturm ging über gans Deutsch land, wie er in dieser Stärke su den Seltenheiten gehörte. Für ben allgemeinen Flugverkehr war Startberbot. Hur mit Mühe.

Mit der D-2600 über Nürnberg. Ankunft auf dem Reichsparteitag 1934 D-2600.

konnte man sich auf den Beinen halten. Alles schüttelte den Kopf, als der Führer die Maschine be- stieg. Doch schon nach wenigen Minutest kämpfte sie sich empor. Aur mühevoll ham die Maschine borwärts, durch Gewitter und Regenböen, Sturm und Schnee. Ott sackte die flaschine ab, daß der Kopf manches Mitfliegenden mit dem Dache in Berührung kam, aber immer ging es gut. Einmal mußte das Flugzeug weit vor dem Ziel unprogrammäßig notlanden. Um S Whr sollte die Versammlung in

Riel beginnen. Um 5 Uhr bekam ich die Nach.

Wahlreise durch Deutschland

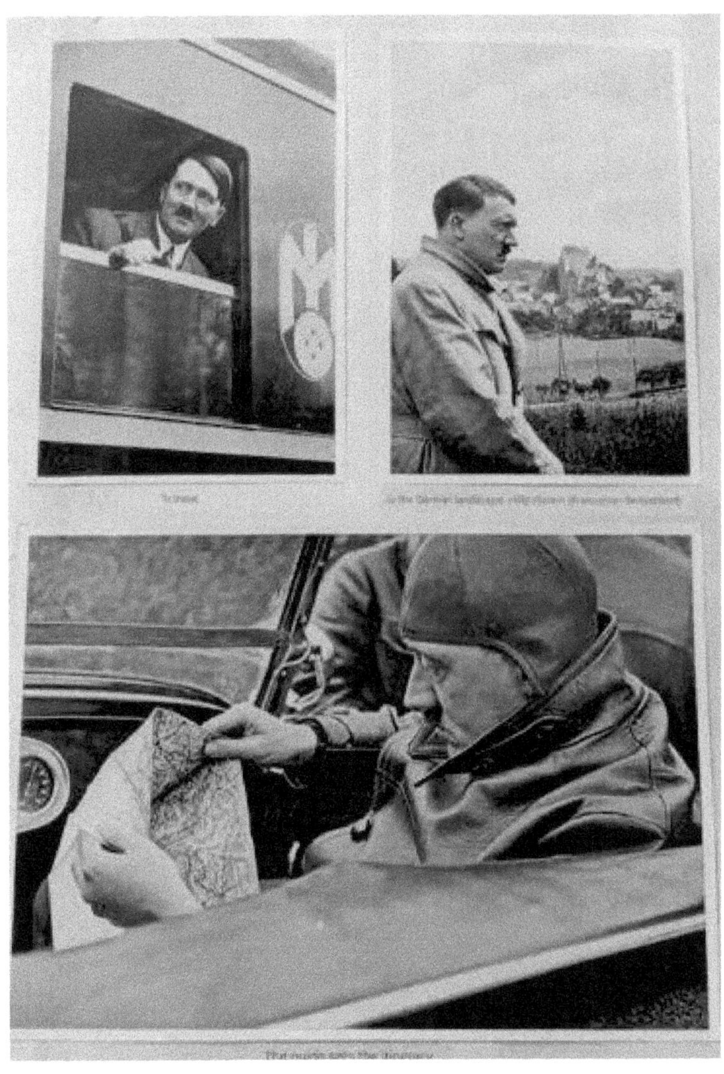

Adolf Hitler

If you were lucky enough to be constantly close to the guide and to experience his many journeys, you would be amazed by the thousands of images that have been captured over the years. You take an unbridled faith in the benefits of such journeys with you, and it is often very heartwarming to be able to experience them all. The guide only makes long journeys in an open car, which he does not close even if it's raining during official events. When his companion gave him the advice, he always replied: "As long as the SA and other formations have to stand in the rain, we can get close too."

Thousands of people witness him, bareheaded and wearing only his brown shirt, inspecting the parade of the SA during the reintegration of the SA, how he spoke to the waiting crowd in the pouring rain after a night flight in Stralsund at 3 a.m., or how he drove through Holstein to the Adolf Hitler Koog in the rain, soaked through, without considering himself, because the SA was also standing in the rain.

On his travels through Germany, the guide prefers the open road. Three black cars appear, and it suddenly becomes clear who is driving past. The children are usually the first to recognize the guide. At that moment, a race with the car starts, and then it is usually no longer a long way to a crowd of people. The alarm spreads through several streets, and finally, we have to stop several times so that the guide can shake hands with the enthusiasts and accept flowers or even sign a few cards. Anyone who, like me, has been driving for 10 years knows that these moments are priceless.

In his first car he already sat next to the driver, after 15 years as Reichs.

We had to hold a rally, drive into the strongholds of our staunch and fierce opponents, often right through the middle of wild battles with the Bolshevik organizations, alongside demonstrations of others. Sometimes, our cars were ambushed by thousands of angry fellow countrymen. But we have seen time and again how, under the Führer's gaze, they suddenly raised their fists, realizing with surprise and joy that this Hitler was completely different from how he had always been described to them. How many misguided German workers then looked for the first time into the eyes of the man they had followed so closely as an opponent, only to become fanatical supporters of his movement all at once. Pure newspaper propaganda, no books alone could have accomplished this miracle. And so, three years after he came to power, he could ask: "Where is the statesman who, like me, need not be afraid to go out among the people after three years in power, just as he did then?"

If his work and government business allow him, the Führer is not only in his office today, but travels out into the country. The leader in Franconia. At the war memorial in Hiltpoltstein (Franconian Switzerland), the JSD.AP. is right in the middle of the people. Then he drives back in his Mercedes and turns up here and there; one day in the Ruhr area, the next in Baden, Württemberg, Saxony, East Prussia, on the edge of the river, in short, there is no region that he doesn't go to at least once. At the wheel of the car, behind the gun window, I hear visibly astonished and enthusiastic exclamations: "The Hitler" or "The Führer is here." Often, people don't even notice who just passed through the city. Only when the column passes by do they realize what has happened as they drive through a Franconian town.

Adolf Hitler

Vickie Boyle &Jessica Diaz

The founding of the party in 1920

When Hitler received the order from the Education Office to attend a meeting of the German Uebriter Party, he did not realize that this evening would become decisive, not just for him. At a Pleinen Sinterstübchen, his "body room" at the Eternederbräu in Munich, he met around 20 to 35 people who were listening to a lecture on economic policy.

There was no talk of a party. Hitler was in a group, a political debating area where the common insecurities, the questionability of every principle, and every idea that left its mark on the period around 1900 became very clear. After all, a brochure that a young worker pressed into Hitler's hand as he was leaving the meeting offered more than the previous evening. The brochure, titled My Political Awakening, was from Anton Drexler, the Munich leader of the Workers' Party. This brochure reflected the struggles of the soul that

Hitler himself had tried to provoke most emphatically during his time in Vienna. The next day, he received the news that he had been accepted into the party, a development that made him both angry and amused.

But he accepted the renewed invitation. It was aimed at the "old Rosenbad," an obscure bar where Hitler got to know the lively group of people who had come together to save the German worker. Yet, amid the clumsiness and non-political propaganda, something captured Hitler's attention: the honest belief that success was possible.

He wanted to fight for the fatherland again against the Marrianana and the Red Revolution from the German author. After two days of struggle, Hitler decided to join the Workers' Party. He received provisional membership certificate No. 7. No one in Munich knew the party, but it was gratifying when they received a few letters and debated for a long time about how to respond.

Every Wednesday, there was a so-called meeting at Café Safteig, and once a week, there was a reception. However, since the entire movement consisted of only seven men, the same people always met in a grim and remote manner. Expanding the group seemed to be Hitler's first goal. If the party was to emerge from anonymity, it needed to grow.

Invitations to meetings were handwritten. Hitler personally delivered eighty of them. But on the evening of the meeting, the old crowd was there again, and there was no one new. Hitler then switched to having the invitation slips typed, and the results improved. The number of attendees rose to eleven, then thirty, seventeen, twenty-three, and finally thirty-four.

A collection of money at one of these meetings provided the opportunity to announce the following in the Munich Observer. And lo and behold: 111 people showed up. It was a huge success. For the first time, Hitler realized he had the gift of speaking to a larger audience, a fact the party chairman had not been able to believe. Hitler's appeal to the attendees' willingness to make sacrifices even raised 300 marks.

This was a fortune for the party. Additionally, after this meeting, a number of young people volunteered, with whom substantial work could be planned. Because once an anti-Marxist party became public in 1919-1920, there were bloody confrontations. The party leadership feared this as well.

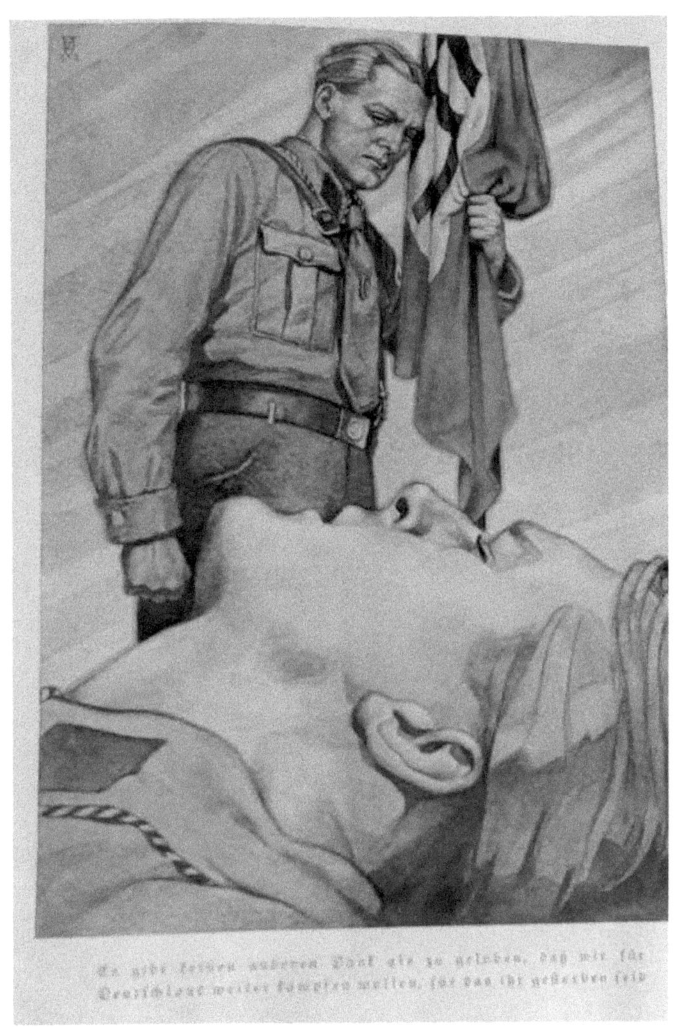
Es gibt keinen anderen Dank als zu geloben, daß wir für
Deutschland weiter kämpfen wollen, für das ihr gestorben seid

They fought for Germany's resurrection, the Fuhrer greets wounded SA men

The Fuhrer sees a clear fighter

Not only the service of the commune, the Reidyo banner, and the center-over associations—these would have been bearable. The RODAP had acquired these people more than once. What was worse, the insidious terror of individual actions and murders was encouraged, incited, begged for, and supported by the officially practiced terror of the senior officers, the police, and the authorities. All of that was no longer an exception. It was as natural, pure, and secret as the fighting style of the underworld, except that this terror from above used the power of the state to suppress the fighting movement.

It began with bans on gatherings and marches, continued with bans on posters and newspapers, and soon, there was no National Socialist newspaper that had not been banned at least once. This fate befell the "Attack" 16 times. Searches of party premises were the order of the day. Marches, open-air gatherings, and demonstrations were forbidden. Leaflets, badges, exercises, and closed member meetings were prohibited. Trucks were stopped if there was even the slightest suspicion that they might be in possession of National Socialists. Election rallies on the radio were banned. Academic freedom was revoked. The police raided the universities. The rubber truncheons, the SA homes—these were the only refuge and place to stay. The camps of unemployed SA men or those threatened with death by the commune were closed. Beds, pictures, tables, chairs, and blankets were thrown onto the street.

Finally, Interior Minister Gröner even banned the entire SA, and they fought for Germany's resurrection. The Führer greeted wounded SA men and forbade the wearing of any badge, any tie, and even the wearing of brown shirts and trousers. But Bi 21 didn't let herself be discouraged. If they took her shirt away, she would march shirtless. Even without a brown shirt, the Führer could see where his people belonged.

Mildly and bluntly, the brave men were boded naked by only more open-minded, more willing to give up and therefore more confident of victory. Finally, the Peruvian police started arresting them. They were brought home by the police wearing a prisoner's cap. The surrender of this prisoner's cap cost them money. Democracy took care of its subjects! Thousands were thrown out of their jobs. Party members were randomly arrested, detained for three days, and then released just as randomly and without trial. When they then wanted to return to their work, they found their place of work gone, deemed as an unjustified absence.

My God, there are so many people crying out for work. The Social Democrats were in charge of the state-owned companies, the Reich companies, the municipal companies, the banks, and firms. They fired the Nazi suspects on orders, threw them out onto the street, and handed them and their families over for ransom. But all this terror, all this persecution—although they could not speak rudely of the movement, they formed a great banik Adolf Stirre. And if they had not piled up the devastation and meditated and followed the hunger and need for food in the morning, they would have sooner lost their lives than given their bread to the Führer and his bride at the Hakensee.

We will not surrender! Goebbels calls to the people from above and into the Zerreriften's hate-filled face from below. And with surrender shouted a movement of a million! Unknown only to his knowing and committed to his leader, the unknown man did his difficult service. He didn't look right or left, day or night; he just went forward and followed his leader blindly and faithfully. Thanks to the heroism of the unknown man, no democratic system came into being. Every weapon was blunted against him.

A trendem Deil Hitler

But the Führer feels how they bravely bite back the pain, how they suffer, and pride and grief that he faces. The handshake with which were to risk their lives, to sacrifice everything, ever the clay? None except Adolf Hitler's movement greeted the wounded in a handshake. The bloodshed guaranteed victory, unbreakable loyalty and means Comrades, just as But it also imposed ever more sacred deligations you have not abandoned the holy cause of the Party. They must never have died in movement, too will never abandon it. From 1930 variant 3 to 1932, the terror increased from foxes you attach to it. I will never sell good week-to-week sacrifices for external gais. There, they lie in hospital beds, mortally wounded, and the Führer has nothing left to do for them except to stand by their bed of pain and send a quick prayer to the Lord that he may preserve life for those who are mortally wounded. The victims of terror and cowardly attacks are great. But they are the tood send from which the Third Reich grew. Where in Germany was there a movement, where was there a leader, where was there an idea for which hundreds of thousands were prepared?

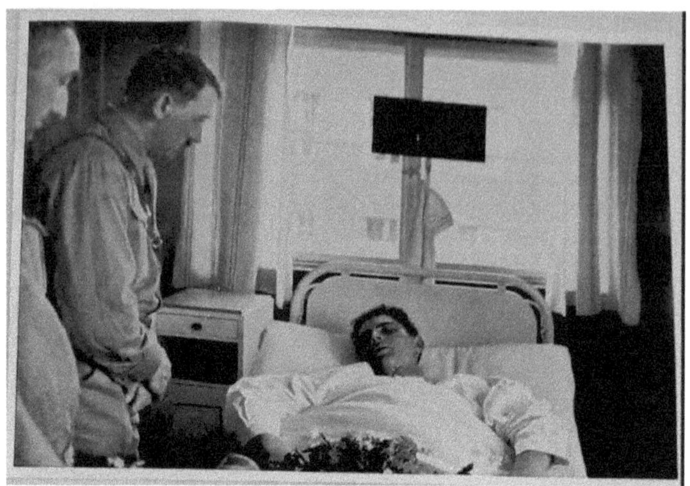

Fallen for Germany's resurrection, Murdered by the communists.

The Fuhrer at the deathbed of a 14-year-old comrade, 1931

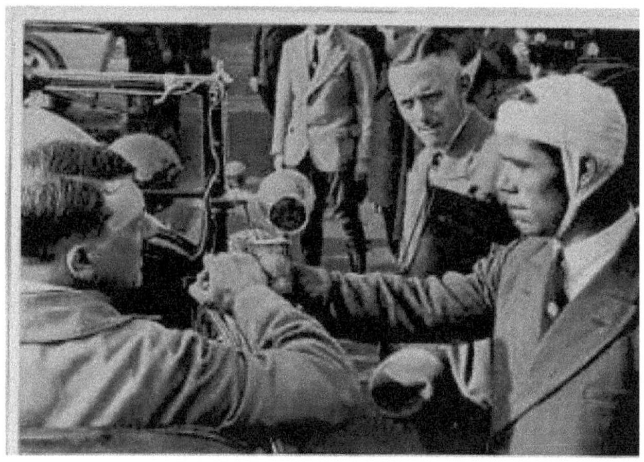

Blood clots of the movement

Chapter Two
Rise to Power

Adolf Hitler: What name in the world could be more prominent than this? In cities and countries across the globe, his name resonates. At the same time, his name is associated with greatness and leadership. Millions of people, not only in Germany (who still travel to him and hope), and even his staunchest opponents must reluctantly acknowledge his outstanding personality. But what does the world really know about him?

He was born on April 20, 1889, in Braunau on the Austrian-German border, on the banks of the Inn. He grew up as one of the most deprived youths among German war immigrants and, after the collapse of 1918, emerged as the leader of the national revolution of 1922, which he led through many difficult years to make it the dominant party in Germany. But how incomplete is the picture that is painted?

To truly understand the life story of the Führer with respect, one must consider the details of his early life. Adolf Hitler, born in Braunau, was raised by his mother in a small, picturesque town. At the age of six, his family moved to Linz, where his father retired. The family settled in Lambach, nestled in the Alps, with a view of the snowy dream landscape, the Höllengebirge and the Zoten mountains. The young boy was deeply influenced by the natural beauty around him. His experiences in this serene environment shaped his future aspirations.

Initially, Hitler aspired to become a painter. He deliberately neglected his school studies but passionately pursued art. He understood the importance of brotherhood and loyalty. His journey took him through various struggles. Despite his fervent desire to be a painter, he found himself diverging towards architecture. However, to pursue this path, he needed to pass the final exams in high school, a challenge he struggled with. His early attempts to enter the art academy were met with setbacks, but his determination remained steadfast.

On May 2, 1014, at the Omneleg in Mansion, right in the middle of the crowd, Wolf Hitler

You learn to recognize Marxism at its roots. Read more willingly and understand how this poison eats away at the soul of the worker. But you can also see how this understanding reveals that only one thing can save a nation: a true nationalism that overcomes the divisive idea of Jewish Marxism.

An immediate request to serve voluntarily in the First Regiment of the Bavarian Reserve Infantry Regiment No. 10, made up of young, enthusiastic volunteers, exemplified this spirit. Adolf Hitler, with undaunted enthusiasm and hard work, served for years, not only as a nationalist but as a dedicated member of this regiment.

If Hitler was initially called up countless times as a member of this unit, he proved his commitment and diligence.

After graduating from Munden in 1912, he became an observant and active student. Hitler spent many happy years in Munich, the vibrant capital of German culture. Then, the outbreak of World War I struck like a bolt of lightning. For him, on the border between Germany and German Austria, there were many options. At this fateful hour, he decided in favor of the Reich and immediately registered as a war volunteer.

Hitler in Zelde

Walker, through the hell of battle, with the importance of countless messages, he found strength in his comrades and depended on them. Through the raging battles, he remained a cold-blooded and determined fighter, ruthlessly seizing opportunities to attack. Once, during a marked opportunity, he and a comrade captured a French soldier.

At the turn of the year 1915/16, the ambitious volunteer who had stormed the young movement, laughing and cheering, gradually transformed through a difficult internal process into a front-line soldier with an indomitable will. In 1910, he was wounded for the first time. By 1917, Adolf Hitler received the Iron Cross.

During these years of incredible struggle for the survival of a people, Adolf Hitler witnessed the German people's heroism without shame. Whenever his path later became difficult, he remembered these comrades, these fighters, and these people. One can never despair of a people who can boast of such individuals and such achievements.

In 1918, his regiment was stationed for the third time in Flanders. By this point, the disintegration at the front had become increasingly noticeable after the munitions workers' strike in the homeland spread to the fighting front. Adolf Hitler never forgave German democracy for this horrific national crime. On October 13, 1918, English artillery bombarded the regimental sector for hours with Yellow Cross grenades, whose poisonous fibers also affected Hitler.

When news of the revolution reached him, it came with the certainty that he would be able to regain honor. At this moment, he vowed to rid the nation of the shame of the revolt. In March, almost healed, he returned to Munich, where he was to examine the events of the revolution. He became a training officer and began his work as a political revivalist.

During this period, he encountered the "German Workers' Party." The party was a small group of barely a dozen men, but Adolf Hitler realized that something significant was happening. After two days of deliberation, the group was reorganized, and the DA became the NSDAP, the National Socialist German Workers' Party. On February 24, 1920, in the great ballroom of the Munich Hofbräuhaus, he announced the party's program, the famous 25 points, which have never changed.

The fight lasted 14 years. Through all the highs and lows, the storm of the movement broke out. The court declared them traitors to the movement and imprisoned them in the Landsberg fortress. There, he wrote his great confession, the story of his life and ideas, encapsulated in the book "Mein Kampf." On December 20, 1924, Hitler left the fortress. On December 21, the work of the NSDAP began on different grounds. This time, the movement became a party, beating its opponents with their own weapons.

On February 24, 1920, the movement, now a party, fought on. The image of Adolf Hitler, once a man with a fanatical love for his people, now shines pure and clear before an entire nation. He remained what he was, a kind, great man dedicated to his people and determined to become the architect of a new Reich. The first steps of this journey were now underway.

Wolf Hitler was wounded in the Beelit Passenger Ship

The First Office of the NSDAP

Hitler did not fear taking the stage in public and preferred it over hiding in the Eberbraukeller. 130 Jews attended an early rally. An attempt to break up the protest was made in Crim. A fortnight later, there was another rally with increasing numbers. Soon, 1,200 to 1,300 people were listening to the speaker, Adolf Hitler.

Unfortunately, the NSDAP initially formed only a small circle within the German Workers' Party. The formulation of the 25 points began not without fierce struggles, but in the end, the superiority of the propaganda leader, Adolf Hitler, prevailed. The Marxist press had already begun to attack the new party. The first hate-filled articles appeared. At foreign meetings, Hitler's supporters began to speak. The movement was no longer unknown. Even though the speakers of the German Workers' Party were constantly shouted down at foreign meetings, it became clear that there were other people besides social democrats who were not Marxists, people who were anything but bourgeois.

In the large hall of the Hofbräuhaus, Harrer resigned from his post, fearing the collapse of the party. Hitler then attacked the assembly with his impetuosity and overcame the reservations of the existing politicians. Leaflets and posters were handed out. The posters, in bloody red, were designed to attract attention and were particularly visible to Marxists, who believed they were being directly challenged by Hitler.

Hitler considered it crucial that the workers on the left, especially those under the influence of Jewish leaders, be drawn away from their current affiliations. He ensured that the party program, which had been prepared over a long period, was finalized and printed.

Then came the memorable February 24, 1920, when, to the cheers of 2,000 people, the first great battle was fought, and the birthday of the National Socialist German Workers' Party was celebrated with the announcement of the program.

A historic corner in the Cafe Sastrig in Munich

Here sat the first seven of the movement

The birth of the NSDAP

The Oberlanders at the Schnerweihe in Munich, 1923

At 2:00 pm, the party's first major parade was scheduled to take place in the Sofbraubans Mo Suler. By a quarter past seven, Arfifaal was filled with anxious anticipation, unsure if he would be able to confront the thronging crowd that had gathered in the wide Paul. Hitler observed that about half of the audience consisted of troops, committees, and independents, not just those he had intended to address. Despite this, he was determined to push forward under any circumstances.

The more powerful, younger members of the party, trained Golbats, took control of the situation, ready to ruthlessly expel any Ochreians at the slightest disturbance. Just minutes after Hitler began speaking, hecklers started to interrupt. The first clashes occurred in the middle of the Gaal. A communist struck a Hitler supporter, knocking him to the ground. In no time, the expulsion operation was underway, and peace was restored. However, the interjections continued to disrupt Hitler's speech as he laid out the Party's main points.

The longer he spoke, the fewer interruptions there were. The noise subsided, and Hitler's warm, florid voice began to resonate throughout the Gaal. Applause erupted and grew louder. When Hitler announced the final of the 25 points and declared to the crowd, "The leaders of the party promise, if necessary with the sacrifice of their own lives, to advocate for the implementation of the above points ruthlessly," thunderous cheers erupted. A group of people stood united before Hitler, inspired by a new conviction, belief, and will—a new purpose. The NSDAP was born.

The new party soon gained valuable allies. Munich Police Chief Pöhner and Oberamtmann Grid openly supported the movement, despite being in conscious opposition to the government, which had already begun to pay more attention to the rising movement. The government even banned the current advertising posters "out of traffic considerations," claiming they caused too many people to gather and obstruct traffic. However, it was clear that the real issue was the provocative content and color of the posters.

The party found confidence in the support of Police Chief Pöhner, whom Hitler described in his book as "a man of granite honesty, anti-feral simplicity, and German straightforwardness, for whom the phrase 'Better dead than slave' was not just a saying but the epitome of his entire being." The same characterization applied to Senior Bailiff Frid, who would go on to become Reich Minister of the Interior a decade later.

In December, Hitler founded the "Völkischer Beobachter," where Dietrich Eckart, the movement's loyal advocate, proclaimed the ideas of National Socialism. Every week, meetings were held in the Hofbräuhaus, and each week, the hall became even more crowded. Hitler's belief that a speech was more impactful than a book received its first confirmation.

The Reds' tactics varied between attempts to silence the entire movement or disrupt its meetings, but since both strategies failed consistently, Hitler managed to win over a whole group of workers from the Red Front.

Hwrite Gefschaftofielle det NEYAP and bes Regt. Mangen,

oberit, Bulidiner, Corneliustrabe ra in Munsten

Soon, the first people were seen running around in windbreakers, each with a fresh armband displaying a black hook gleaming against a white background. These were the Gaalshus— young, daring lads, foremen, and goldards—who were unafraid of harsh beatings and who guaranteed peace and order during the meetings. They were determined fellow partisans, ready to counter terror with terror, each depending on which form of terror would prove better and more decisive.

In the summer of 1920, the organization of this force took on a more solid form. By the spring of 1921, it had been divided into PAF and PAF units, each consisting of hundreds of members who automatically divided themselves into smaller groups. The organization began to take shape.

At this point, a party symbol—a party flag—became inevitable. Nobody understood the power of symbols better than Hitler. A movement, a community, a people, or a state without a symbol to ignite hearts—a symbol to which they could direct all their longing, pride, and enthusiasm—is lifeless and, therefore, ineffective.

More than anything, the red banners or red cockades had helped Marxism because an idea, a belief, needs visible expression. After several attempts, Hitler created the swastika flag as a combination: the red flag with a white circle and a forward-spinning swastika, a symbol of truly violent momentum and striking beauty.

In midsummer 1920, the new flag was presented to the public for the first time.

In February 1921, the party saw the introduction of a new armband worn by the Gaalschub group, symbolizing their affiliation with the growing movement. This development marked a period of significant changes within the organization. The party held a significant meeting in the Munich Circus, which stirred considerable attention and protest from various factions. Many attendees took to their feet, and by July 1945, Hitler had assumed sole leadership of the movement.

On November 4th, a long-awaited separation from the Commune occurred. Hitler, who had been active in the Belbräu establishment, prepared for the event with meticulous planning. The rally was scheduled to start an hour after Hitler learned of the preparations. Despite challenges, Hitler managed to secure a spacious room for the gathering. The meeting proceeded without major disruption until a group of Reds attempted to storm the venue. Hitler, seizing the moment, rallied the crowd with a cry of "Freedom," which turned the assembly into a chaotic scene of roars and screams.

In the aftermath, the extreme poverty and discontent of the time continued to fuel unrest. Hitler's departure that evening marked the establishment of the German Sturmabteilung (SA). This new formation, characterized by their distinctive brown uniforms, became synonymous with the party's growing influence. The SA moved from gathering to gathering, becoming a powerful force with a life of its own.

The movement's symbol, the hook-joy armband, and their organized, disciplined approach became central to their identity. By then, the party had gained significant traction in Munich, with the SA becoming a well-established entity. However, the organization faced challenges in maintaining discipline and training a militarily skilled force, as the primary focus remained on political education rather than military training.

Adolf Hitler did not see the party's symbols merely as representations of democracy but as embodiments of the rule of law and political discipline. He believed that a disciplined political system was essential to guide and inspire the youth. In a dramatic display of power and organization, Hitler orchestrated a large parade, where eight hundred Nazis marched into Coburg with flags flying and bands playing. This spectacle was intended to demonstrate the movement's strength and resolve.

Hitler articulated his vision in his book, emphasizing that the movement needed not just a few daring warriors, but hundreds of thousands of dedicated fighters. He argued that the struggle should not be waged in isolated camps but through grand processions that showcased the movement's might. The future, he asserted, would see National Socialism ruling not just the streets but eventually the state itself.

Thus, Hitler did not model the SA's training on traditional military standards but on the needs of the party. He also ensured that their uniforms were distinct from those of the old army. The first large-scale march of the SA occurred during a protest rally in Munich against the implementation of the Republic Law. The impressive display of several hundred units, with waving banners, received a rousing reception from the crowd. The march was marked by violent clashes with opposing forces, resulting in significant bloodshed.

By 1922, the NSDAP extended its reach beyond Munich. Hitler was invited to a German Day festival in Coburg, and he brought eight hundred men as his escort. Upon arrival, the festival organizers had a prearranged agreement with the Coburg Social Democrats that prohibited any Nazis from marching. The SA faced serious attacks upon arrival, and the police, unable to control the situation, confined the SA members to a cellar.

Hitler demanded that the doors be opened, but the police complied only slowly. As a result, the SA eventually had to retreat. The lack of response from the National Socialists to insults and provocation led to increased violence from the Commune, culminating in a devastating counterattack by the SA. The violence resulted in significant casualties and severe attacks on individual National Socialists. By the following morning, the red terror in Coburg was quelled, marking a significant victory for the Nazis.

A little piece of the movement, Soburg 1902

The National Socialist Party faced significant challenges, but by May 1, 1923, the situation had changed. The party had faced intense opposition, and by that date, it was clear that their previous struggles were over. The building was filled with a breath-taking atmosphere of excitement and anticipation.

The time for action had arrived. Adolf Hitler clearly defined what the party should be: just as they had once appeared dangerous to their opponents, they had to ensure that no opportunity was missed to discourage visits to National Socialist meetings in the Crimea or to prevent them through repression. Only by expanding their reach could they ensure the persistence of the movement and gain the public attention and respect deserved by those who, when attacked, stand firm.

The guiding principle for training the stormtroopers (SA) was to make them not only formally trained but also unshakably committed representatives of National Socialist ideals. This training aimed to instill the highest degree of discipline.

The organization was not meant to resemble a bourgeois military or a secret society. After the collapse in 1923 and the re-establishment of the party and the SA in 1925, the tried-and-true principles of SA training were immediately reintroduced. Based on these steadfast principles, the movement achieved victory after victory.

The sustainability of this approach became evident only a few years later, when Coburg became the first city to elect a National Socialist mayor. A short strike by railway staff, who refused to return a special train to Munich, was resolved within a quarter of a year. The train carrying the victorious SA left on time. At the first party congress of the movement on January 27, Hitler was able to present a solidly united party, battle-tested and prepared for future challenges.

The first four standards, adorned with the movement's national emblem—the soaring eagle and the wreathed swastika—were handed over to the 21st. The first hundreds of members were now wearing the new uniform: a wind cap, which had become known as the "21st hat," and a windbreaker with a belt and armband.

Throughout the year, the storm detachments led by Göring defeated the Red `Terror in numerous Bavarian cities. The leader of the Munich Regiment was First Lieutenant Brückner. The country was systematically cleansed, and freedom of expression was restored. One Red stronghold after another fell to National Socialist propaganda.

However, in March 1923, a shift occurred in the development of the SA as a political fighting force. The French occupation of the Ruhr area saw hundreds of brave SA men meet heroic deaths under French bayonets. By September, passive resistance had collapsed. While German youth fought valiantly in the Ruhr area, Marxism betrayed them to the French.

First Nazi party rally in Munich in 1923

The party was founded on February 24th. On January 27, 1923, it joined the first Reich Party.

What a long way had been covered in these three years. When the party started, it had nothing but a dark room. Slowly, the room got electric light, and even slower, a telephone. A few rooms and a table were acquired. Finally, a man named Schüßler took over the management. At the end of Nad's service, he came to the shop from 6 to 8 to complete the most necessary work. A small Abler typewriter, which he owned, was purchased by the party in long installment payments. A small coffee cupboard was acquired to store membership cards. In November, the move to the Gornelius building took place.

Here, there were three rooms available. Business traffic began to pick up, and a separate counter room became necessary. Hitler's old regimental comrade, Amann, who later headed the Franz Scher publishing house, took over the party's management.

He was neither known nor feared by Baben Modhten, nor did he harm anyone's hair. Like a threatening, heavy storm cloud, he stood in front of the city of Munich, a visible force to keep order in case the Marxists were revealed to cause disorder. However, Hitler was determined to take ruthless action. The Reich could not afford Marxist power in Munich in 1923.

But the Marxists understood the threat perfectly. They knew better than the harmless bourgeoisie that the National Socialists would never strike unless they were attacked. They understood that the SA only took physical action when it was attacked and only took up arms when confronted with armed force.

They also discovered that the SA showed no consideration and had so far been able to deal with any kind of terror. The gentlemen on the left still remembered very clearly the situation in Coburg and Niederbayern, in Landshut and the party conference. They even remembered the battle in the Hofbräuhaus.

Thus, they refrained from provoking. Marxism did not march through the streets of Munich. The streets remained empty. The Reds no longer dared to assert their supposed right to the streets. So, the A and the Fatherland Associations marched into Munich. The weapons remained on the Oberwiesenfeld. There was no need for them. The defeat of the left-wing parties was also full of pomp.

The gentlemen on the left still remembered very clearly the situation in Coburg and Nieberbayern, in Landehut and the party conference. They even remembered the battle in the Hofbräuhaus.

By this time, the party had established a stable financial footing, with income and expenditure balanced. Every resource was utilized to ensure the party's achievements and sustain its growth. Under the energetic leadership of Hitler, the party had secured a firm administrative base. Despite the party's internal success, it faced significant challenges from the Bavarian state government.

The government was opposed to the party congress and its meetings, particularly in Munich's largest halls. They sought to restrict public demonstrations and impose bans. This strategic move was meant to either force Hitler to comply with restrictions or to find ways to sidestep the bans, depending on his reaction.

However, Hitler's determination prevailed. Despite the state's attempts to obstruct the congress, the event proceeded, albeit in a modified format. Instead of being held in a single large hall, it was spread across twelve locations, but still managed to make a significant impact. A large image was displayed, and thousands gathered, adorned with flowers and windbreakers, pledging their loyalty to Hitler.

The party congress was a resounding success for Hitler. The number of party members surged, and the administrative office struggled to keep up with the influx of new applications. In the evening, all twelve meeting locations were packed well before the scheduled time. The first edition of the "Völkischer Beobachter" appeared as a daily newspaper shortly afterward, with Fred Rosenberg as editor-in-chief. This marked a significant step in the party's propaganda efforts.

The successful congress demonstrated the power and appeal of the movement, which had previously only been an emerging force. By contrast, Marxism, which had briefly held sway, was seen as increasingly weak in the face of the Nazi rise.

In response to the growing influence of the NSDAP, the government continued to react cautiously. Although the state authorities allowed some demonstrations, they were vigilant and took measures to prevent any potential violence. On May 1st, the authorities surrounded the Oberwiesenfeld with soldiers to preempt any Marxist unrest, although the anticipated confrontation did not materialize. The NSDAP did not stage any dramatic actions, and the day passed without significant incident.

This strategic approach allowed the party to consolidate its position and showcase its growing strength without provoking unnecessary conflicts.

Dolphin and Nation

There are nets of people. Uniformed, they stand tall and upright through the door. Then Ale, the staff, is on the Bebium. A terrible storm breaks through. The crowd is released. Cities behind them, he speaks, but words fail him. Then, he raises the gun at the target. A note tallies their movements. Enbenbeell Eltung of the Gramsen politics. The horse reflects on the monarchy. Geller Cali: Give thanks in this brooding of two difficulties at the table. Shither leaves. Then Messrs. von Kabe, von Kabe, and Loffee discuss the National Revolution in Mindien, 1923.

Hitler raises his hand: "The national revolution has broken out." He doesn't get any further. A huge outburst of cheering tears his words to pieces. Yes, now they all know why they have come here this evening. Now they know what they have been waiting for so long. They were waiting for exactly these words: "The national revolution has broken out." It is a scene of incredible force. Kaht, pale and trembling, and Geißer and Lossow go into the next room with Hitler. Meanwhile, the A arrests the gentlemen from the Bagrian government: Kolling, Schweiger. Then Hitler appears again and announces the list of ministers for the national revolution: State Governor von Kahr, Prime Minister Pöhner, Reichswehr.

A huge crowd gathers in front of the town hall. When Hitler returns, Ludendorff has the daring to be released. At this hour, the station of the 19th Infantry Regiment stands. General State Commissioner Kahr, General Colonel Geißer reject Hitler's putsch. Participation in the Bürgerbräu meeting is invalid. The revolution has been betrayed. An hour later, M. Kahr dissolves the revolution. In addition, the Oberland Association and the Reich flag were added. Kahr lets the troops march. Against Marxism? Against the Bolshevik threat? Against the Social Democratic government? No!

WON!=
THESE MEN FELL ON
9 NOVEMBER 1923 IN FRONT
OF THE FELDHERRN HALL
AND IN THE COURTYARD OF
THE MINISTRY OF WAR IN
FAITHFUL BELIEF IN THE
RESURRECTION OF THEIR PEOPLE

=AND YOU HAVE

Freiferpe Oberland marches to
Adolf Hitler after laying the foundation stone of the Befreienendenmals

But Hitler was still in Munich, and he threw the movement—the whole party, everything he had at his disposal—into the scales for Germany, for the unity of the Reich, against separatism, as well as against Marxism and Bolshevism. On November 3rd, a Berlin newspaper reported that Kabro and Loffewa had "clearly broken away from Hitler." There was no need for this report. Everything must be decided in just a few days. A terrible tragedy hangs over Germany. Who will bring relief? Will it lead to success or ruin? Nobody knows.

November 8th sees Munich in a fever of joy. Everyone is hoping that a decision will be made now, one way or another, and they hope that this decision will be called Hitler. Since he liberated the city from red terror on May 1st, Munich belongs to him. Wherever a Hakenkreuz flag appears, everyone greets it. Where is the Red Yellowshush? He hasn't been seen in the last few weeks, but he's lurking in his holes. And tomorrow is November 10th.

The Bund Oberland marches into the city. In their traditional Bavarian costume—shorts, jackets thrown over them, the swastika armband on their arms—they rouse the people of Munich to tumultuous enthusiasm. Mr. von Kabr has called a meeting in the Bürgerbräukeller for the evening of November 8th. Apparently, some business organizations are organizing the meeting, but it is not entirely safe. The meeting is overcrowded. No one knows yet what is going to happen. All we know is that a decision was made five years ago. Today, another decision is at hand. Everyone feels it. Kahr is introduced to the crowd. Applause breaks out. Kahr speaks. "From the people to the nation" is the theme. To which nation?

No one in the audience has any idea what is going on during Kahr's lackluster speech. On the streets of Munich, the revolution is developing. The uprising is beginning. The swastika flags are fluttering on the streets of Munich, and where the swastika is flying, that is Germany—whole and undivided. Cars rumble in front of the Bürgerbräu. The shock troops sit at the command on the street, giving a few half-whispered commands. At Gendlingertorplatz, Am Stachus, at Marienplatz, columns march. A car races to the Bürgerbräukeller. "This talk of the Danube Federation is madness.

Do we want to see the work of the Commune, the work of France, continue?" The car screeches to a halt. Kahr is still talking.

Hitler's Shock Troops, 1993

Vickie Boyle &Jessica Diaz

Hitler Trial

The 20th of February is a sad day. In the bloody crowds, people are crowded together in uniforms, police in the Munich People's Court. In the building that used to be the war school, the trial against Hitler and his comrades for treason takes place. Panicked riders, barbed wire on the approach road, passport checks, weapons checks, gun control. His police, blue police, another operation. The presbytery is crowded into the sober courtroom, all the audience seats are occupied. When the defendants appear, a heated debate ensues. No one pays any attention to the court. There they are, the defendants, smiling. They stand tall and broad, showing no fear. Hitler wears the Iron Cross on his chest. Next to him is Frick, very excited, along with Pobner, Kriebel, and all the others. It is a select dock. (One rack after another full of characters.) Finally, the chairman opens, "Mr. Adolf Hitler?" The leader bows slightly. "First of all, I would like to ask you to give us a comprehensive description of your life's journey." Very good. That is exactly what Hitler wants. The leader's request is like a cue, and Hitler speaks. He speaks for four and a half hours. The courtroom sinks, the walls fade away, and only one man stands there, and hundreds of thousands to millions listen to him. This is by no means an accused man; this is a relentless accuser, and his words burn like flames. Hitler describes his life—Vienna, the hunger, the hard work, Marxism, the so-called workers' leaders, terror, old Austria, the international Jews.

"As an anti-Semite and sworn enemy of Marxism, I leave Vienna." The words resonate like a clap of thunder in the room. Quietly, Hitler continues. He speaks of the war, speaks of the revolt of 1918. He doesn't need to say much about that time. Everyone in the room still remembers them—the men with rifles slung across their backs, the looters and marauders, the backpack Spartans and Soviet republicans, the false sailors who desecrated the glory of the fleet, the slayers and sadists. He speaks of the battles of the first seven and the assault divisions, of the battle in the Hofbräuhaus, and of the day in Coburg. As he does so, his voice rises, becoming sharp and cutting.

"The terror from the left can only be countered with even more severe measures," he declares. Then, the room starts to rattle. All those in the hall can no longer hold back. "Yes," says a barman, and he is applauded. But now it truly begins. All of that was just a prelude, groundwork—now comes the politics of the last few months, the national revolution, the betrayal of Mr. von Kahr, the shots at the Feldherrnhalle. What was it like with the Kahr government? Was the Bavarian troops' oath of allegiance to Munich a coup d'état against the Reich or not? The accusations rain down on Mr. von Kahr like a storm: "If someone in an army of five divisions holds one in his hand and rebels against the army commander, then he must either risk his life, or he is just a miserable traitor." Applause breaks out again; the spectators give up the futile attempt to calm him down.

"I have," Hitler shouted, "two days before the coup, issued the orders that on November 8th at exactly half past eight, the national government would be proclaimed. I would never have made this decision if I had not been sure that Lossow, Kahr, and Seisser also wanted to eliminate the current situation. Would it have been madness if I had done so without knowing the others' intentions?"

"If I have committed treason, then in my opinion, there is no treason against the traitors of 1918. But if I have committed high treason, then Mr. von Kahr, Mr. von Lossow, and Mr. Colonel Seisser have done the same, and I am very surprised that they have not been tried alongside me." Thunderous applause rages through the hall. But it is not over yet. The decisive statement is still missing, the proud, manly declaration that the future and history will call against the miserable present: "The judges of this state may judge us for our actions. But history, as the goddess of higher truth and better law, will one day tear this judgment apart with a smile to acquit us of all guilt and atonement." Only then does the cheering become enormous.

More than once, a man accused of treason has pleaded before his judges. And now the comrades come. Dr. Weber speaks of Kahr's policy, reporting that he wanted to create his own Bavarian currency. This proves the double-edged policy of this State Commissioner General and sheds light on his dark plans. On November 6, Kahr declared that he was in complete agreement with Hitler.

On November 9th, the name of the party leader Hubert and his wife Deim is mentioned. Negotiations with the Arangejen in Parma, Wiesbaden, and Bourbon are scheduled. The name of the party circle leader of the federalists is also mentioned. Footnotes pile up about rumors of conflagration, but only on the 3rd of March. Belli about Beetridiger, the famous la Ask Kabre, Lofoten, and Pai Bere about Morbes and Oedurrrots on ready-made orders. This leads to wild speeches. The term "November Criminal" is mentioned. Hitler condemned the investigation into political conflicts. He stated, "I have no objections to the November attacks. That was my report and will be my report, and if you don't regret it, so will be the case in the future."

History shines a light on the court case, and then Kahr has to fight. The defenders rush off: "Why don't you have the Reichsbefehle? Why in Bavaria did you not command the Bavarian troops? Why did you confiscate the gold from the Reichsbank in Nuremberg? Why did you want to fight in Thuringia? The wrestling was already completely over on November 6th. Who did you want to fight against? Why did you tell a publisher in Stuttgart that you couldn't wait any longer? Why?... Why? Why?..." Kahr doesn't answer. He can't remember! Kahr doesn't even dare to defend himself. He only answers a secondary question, and his answer is immediately interpreted as a move to evade the truth. As he leaves the courtroom, a wide gap forms in front of him. The people avoid him as if he were a plague victim. Many turn away as Kahr passes before them. Not even a glance should reach this man. They don't even want to look at him. With each passing day, Hitler is becoming more of an accuser than the accused. It became clear to the court that Kahr wanted to carry out a coup—not the Hitler Putsch, but a truly treasonous plot to break Bavaria away from Germany. That was clear. And why Hitler had intervened, why the party had looked to the summit, was also clear.

On March 31st, when the verdict is to be announced, Munich resembles an army camp. The police do not trust the population. The defenders of the accused are showered with thunderous cries of "Heil" wherever they appear. They can hardly make their way through the crowd. The crowd gathers around them, thinking that these men should be brought to the court of the Belt. It's a scene at Pelip. The police can be seen very clearly; no one is allowed near the river. They drive in armored wagons, and those who sit far away can still see us. In the Schlossmem, ifo Monden, the police are in a state of high alert. And waiting on the paths. Finally, the verdict is announced: Hitler, Weber, and Kriebel receive five years in prison with parole. Wagner, Frick, and others get one year each. As the verdict is read, the courtroom bursts into unbridled jubilation. The fans sweep over the pitch, and the verdict comes. This justifies Hitler completely. For a man who thinks and feels German like Hitler, spending over four and a half years on the ground voluntarily fled...

a fan of the republic, shooting, because of the ID fung..." The hall greets every gasp with unbridled applause. The police sit sullenly next to the glowing confession of a person.

Hitler in the fortress cell in Landsberg, 1924

Re-foundation of the Party

Hitler left the Canbebeeg fortress, a site of national significance, on December 20, 1934. The head of the institution had issued a biased directive, but Hitler, ever the determined nationalist, pressed on.

After another confrontation, Rüdfebt and Stribeit saw Hitler persist with his mission. He did not allow himself even a day of rest. "In five years, we will have built the foundations for our future," he declared. By February 27th, the movement had gained enough momentum to be advertised openly. Around 3,000 people packed into the Hofbrauhaus hall, with tens of thousands more standing outside. Not even police baton charges could disperse them. Inside, the hall buzzed with excitement. The Führer was back, and all his loyal followers from the past flocked to him once more.

However, the police, who had taken a particular interest in this meeting, forbade Hitler from speaking. There was no option to appeal this decision, leaving Hitler furious. Meanwhile, the Bavarian People's Party and the entire Weimar Republic were feeling the pressure, but the Nazi party continued to grow day by day, rendering the ban on speeches almost meaningless. True, mass gatherings were impossible to hold, but it was perhaps more important to first train the newly revived party members, to instill in them the eternal principles of the movement in closed meetings, and to create an unbreakable guard. Soon enough, the ban on speeches was lifted.

In July 1926, the movement's 2nd Reich party conference took place in Weimar. What a difference compared to the first conference two years prior! Back then, there was feverish tension, fueled by the spirit of the post-war years, the struggles in Upper Silesia, and the Ruhr crisis. Now, after a year of diligent work and unwavering faith, the party's prospects had grown significantly.

10,000 people attended the conference. Workers from the Ruhr spent 48 hours in poorly heated train cars, gathering their meager provisions just to see Hitler. They came from all over Germany, mingling with the bourgeoisie. The presence of workers, especially from the Ruhr, surprised many. Could national socialism really attract the working class? The bourgeoisie was skeptical, but the party saw it differently, recognizing the potential to break into the workers' front.

The left-wing parties became alarmed, responding with their own defensive strategies. Marxism, in its many shades, united against Hitler's movement, realizing the existential threat it posed. Marxism organized a fierce defensive struggle, employing the same brutal tactics it had used against the bourgeoisie: terror, attacks, and work boycotts. However, what Marxism didn't anticipate was that these methods, effective against the bourgeoisie, would not work against the National Socialists.

Vickie Boyle &Jessica Diaz

Munich People's Court

I consider the contribution of Julius Schaub.

The record commands that Adolf Hitler, born on April 20, 1889, is to be kept in custody following the current sentence for the execution of his prison sentence of five years for the crime of high treason. The time served in custody—two months and two weeks—will be taken into account. Munich, April 1, 1924, at 10:00 AM. The chairman: Signed [signature]. As short and concise as this order for admission may sound, the words "years of the fortress" contain an incredibly long time, especially for a man who only wanted the best—the freedom of his people.

It was on April 1, 1924, that Adolf Hitler passed through the Landsberg prison gate for the first time—not as a prisoner on remand, but as a person sentenced by a people's court. The barred fortress room that took him in was only poorly equipped, with an iron bed, a mattress, a woolen blanket, a small table, a bedside table, and two chairs. Through the barred windows, one could see the wonderful meadows and fields of Landsberg lying beyond the five-meter-long fortress wall. From time to time, the stillness was interrupted by the ringing of rifles when the guard was relieved or by the clattering of keys as the overseer made his rounds. And in this world of loneliness, isolated from the rest of humanity, surrounded only by his loyal fellow fighters and fellow prisoners, the Führer created his great work, "Mein Kampf."

So, April 20th came, on which Adolf Hitler celebrated his 35th birthday. If the detractors at the time believed that the imprisonment of Adolf Hitler would end the movement and that his followers would abandon him, they were proven wrong by the Landsberg post office on this very day. Never before had so many letters, celebratory messages, and packages of love been brought to the fortress prisoner Adolf Hitler. The most beautiful flowers decorated the birthday room, gifts from friends and loyal supporters arrived for weeks and weeks, and the number continued to grow. The number of prisoners in the fortress had increased to 32 men, marking each day with courage and, at times, desolation.

Ever since Hummel had grinned at his face, Boch had always been outside with his family, friends, business associates, and much more. Some people came when they saw a picture through the visitors, who met in green, flower-filled meadows to give thanks to their loved ones. When evening came, those close to him gathered around to give comfort and hope as they read from the book he was creating, bringing faith, confidence, and solace to their hearts. Hitler worked and wrote with great dedication day after day. The other comrades grouped themselves into different commandos—some became ground workers under the trusted hand of their comrade Hamm, who had departed so early, laying paths. Others devoted themselves to gardening, still others made firewood. Everyone found a way to pass the time through work. In the evening, they all gathered in the playground to stretch their limbs before going to bed.

Months passed, and Christmas was just around the corner—Christmas behind iron bars for the first time. The generals had already racked their brains about how Christmas would go. On December 19th, at 12:00 PM, when the fortress inmates had already gone to sleep, the director of the prison appeared in person before Adolf Hitler and brought the joyous Christmas message that he was free. On the morning of December 20th, the Führer gathered his friends around him, handed over command to his current deputy, Rudolf Hess, and said goodbye to each one personally with the promise to do everything possible to ensure that they, too, would soon regain their long-sought freedom. But as he returned to the people, the fight began again.

The breeder leaves Arstung Landsberg. 1924

Weimar 1926. Hitler Party Congress of the newly formed party

March through Weimar, June 1926
(from left to right: Schwarz, Adolf Hitler, Rosenberg,
Heinemann, Feder, Heß, Albrecht)

Ritter von Epp, Bavaria's most popular war hero the
liberator of Munich from the red terror, today Imperial Statholder
of Bavaria

Berlin remains loyal. "Troy Berbot is dead!" is the jubilant motto of the day. The party conference brought together a hundred thousand people. They came from all over—in cars and trucks, on gondolas and bicycles, on foot and in long columns of motorcycles—and they filled the city with enthusiasm and the anticipation of a change that was to come. This party conference was a first triumph. It was a battle won.

As night fell on the last day, a sea of fire poured through Nuremberg. Thousands, tens of thousands, hundreds of thousands of torches swayed through the night to greet the Führer, forming a huge fiery snake that rolled across the city. The marches thundered and roared, the salutes echoed, and an entire city declared its support for the swastika. The lights shone like will-o'-the-wisps.

Sun lamps, brought by the rubble workers from their mines, lit up to greet the workers and the German labor leaders. Every citizen, every guest, was decorated with lights. The flags of the Reich flew all over Nuremberg. The brutish press hyped the demonstration to over a hundred thousand, but they certainly couldn't help doing so. Yet, they didn't truly understand it. That was left to foreign countries, to the Italians. The fascists had a better eye for what was new in Europe. They had their own revolution from this new era behind them. The late August days came to a close with great celebration. The Führer had achieved great things.

Adolf Hitler

Storm Song of the Germans

Storm! Storm! Storm! The serpent is loose, the worm of hell! Folly and lies have broken his chains, and he comes for the gold in the hideous bed! Red as if with blood, the sky is in flames, and the levers crash together terribly. The chapel is crashing down, too! The drake howls and whips them into pieces! Ring for the storm, come now or never! Germany, awake!

Storm! O tower! Storm! Ring the gold from tower to tower, ring the men, the old men, the boys, ring the sleepers from their tombs, ring the girls down from their beds, ring the mothers from their cradles. Let it roar, let the air ring with rage and the thunder of vengeance! Ring the dead from their graves, Germany, awake!

Storm! Storm! O tower! Ring the bells from tower to tower. Ring until the squires begin to swear. Judas appears to win the kingdom, ring until the lustful ones turn red, all around, there is burning, torture, and killing. Ring until the earth rears up under the thunder of saving vengeance. Woe to the people who still dream today! Germany, awake!

Dietrich Eckart

Reichstag election of 20 May 1928

Nuremberg Before the War

On the eve of the war, thirty thousand men gathered in Nuremberg. Among them were five thousand partisans, representing a quarter of the nationalists in the region. These included a hundred dedicated fighters and propagandists who tirelessly spread and explained Hitler's ideas to the wavering, the believers, the desperate, and the misguided Germans. They worked relentlessly because, in the Nazi Party, there were no passive members.

The Challenge to Other Parties

The other political parties faced a daunting challenge: naked, brute force. They contended with the power of the police, the rubber truncheons, the judges, the cowardly acts of robbery and murder, economic terror, intellectual blockades, and deaths from hunger and misery. When the Berlin SA (Sturmabteilung) returned home, they were arrested at the city limits, following orders from a Jewish police vice-president—a figure whom the nationalist Berliners had begrudgingly expelled at great cost.

The Question of Weapons

Did the Brownshirts (SA) have weapons? The Führer had forbidden it, but the question lingered. Despite the Führer's clear command that fighting was legal, the police repeatedly searched the

SA headquarters, yet each search yielded no results. Meanwhile, the Communists were not subjected to the same scrutiny. Shots rang out, leaving men dead on the pavement, but the source of these shots remained unclear. The police of Berlin could not or would not explain.

The Year 1927 and Beyond

As 1927 drew to a close, the political climate remained tense. On May 20, 1928, the National Socialists managed to secure only 12 seats out of 491 in the Reichstag. The newspapers rejoiced at what they saw as a complete defeat—a tiny, almost insignificant minority compared to the nearly 500 representatives of the people. The sentiment was that Hitler would never come to power. Yet, one wonders if the gentlemen from the left and the democratic center had already begun to sense that the National Socialists might soon hold more influence than they dared admit.

Reor Party Day in Nuremberg 1929 The Führer goes to the Congress

Vickie Boyle &Jessica Diaz

The Brown House

Here's a refined version of your passage:

The movement has grown significantly and requires a strict leadership structure and a central location to manage its many offices and departments. These various units are essential for handling the diverse tasks of the party. The member card index also needs ample workspace to ensure there are no delays in the work, which must be efficiently organized.

Flag Hall in the Brown House in Munich

The Führer's study in the Brown House in Munich

The growing movement necessitated the establishment of numerous rooms to accommodate various departments: the judiciary, prize administration, coffee administration, and the leadership team, all of which required ample space to manage the increasing volume of daily mail. The advertising, propaganda, and organization departments also needed dedicated areas to function efficiently. To meet these demands, the Führer decided to acquire a building for the party in Munich.

He chose a modest, old palace on Berenner Street in the Bavarian capital, which could be converted into an administrative headquarters at a relatively low cost. The building was neither over-decorated nor ostentatious; instead, it was plain and dignified. After renovation, its elegant, well-structured simplicity became even more apparent. The Führer's commitment to preserving valuable elements like floors, staircases, and ceilings under challenging conditions was a key consideration, and Munich architect Professor Trooft executed this vision brilliantly.

The Führer, who had once aspired to be an architect in Vienna, designed many aspects of the building himself. His influence extended to the choice of furniture, ceiling designs, and staircase railings, resulting in a blend of beautiful yet simple effects. The building, soon to be known as the "Brown House," would become an imposing five-story structure that would set a new architectural standard. It was simple yet authentic and monumental, reflecting both the party and its leader.

Contrary to the left-wing press's exaggerated claims of opulence—such as gold banisters, extravagant drapes, and an Orientally decorated study—Hitler found amusement in the absurdity of these reports. The left-wing media, obsessed with the supposed excesses of their political opponents, could only imagine such splendor. In reality, the Führer had not indulged in such luxuries, and the building was a reflection of practicality rather than extravagance.

The Brown House in Munich is the destination of many SA men from the Reich
Im Nafine with the Zührer

From Adolf Hitler: Mein Kampf

People are not liberated by inaction, but through sacrifice. The most fundamental right in the world is the freedom to speak, a right that must be nurtured by the sacrifices one makes for their land. The most significant sacrifice is one's own blood shed for this earth. Religious teachings and institutions must remain inviolate for the political leader; otherwise, they risk becoming mere reformers rather than true politicians.

Historically, what was successfully Germanized was the land acquired by our ancestors with the sword and settled by German farmers. The state is not an end in itself but a means—a prerequisite for the development of a higher human culture, though not its cause. True culture arises from a race capable of it. Loving one's people is proven through the sacrifices one makes for them. For us, the state is merely a form; the essence lies in the nation, the people, and their sovereign interests.

The success of an idea depends on the extent to which propaganda has resonated with the populace and the strength and unity of the organization championing it. A National Socialist worker must understand that national economic prosperity directly impacts their own material well-being. Similarly, a National Socialist employer must recognize that the happiness and satisfaction of their employees are crucial for their economic success. Both employees and employers are representatives and trustees of the entire national community.

Pride in one's people should come from the honor of being a citizen of this nation, even in humble roles, rather than holding high status in a foreign land. The German army is meant not to preserve tribal peculiarities but to foster mutual understanding and adaptation among all Germans. Once Marxism is defeated in Germany, its chains will be broken forever.

The party laughed, and when strangers came into the house, they looked in amazement at the yellow sea railings. When they caught sight of the simple white railing, which was decorated with a cross-shaped beacon, they had to look at it skeptically. The golden sea railing was underneath, and it had only been covered with poison to conceal its true nature.

The secret Stoffwerke building rises above a high ground floor. A few steps lead to the entrance, which is decorated on the right and left with the movement's national emblem on a trembling board. In the vestibule, where visitors register, the movement's flags are kept on a flagpole. Their bright red cloth shines into the dim hall, festively greeting visitors. In front of it stands a bust of Bismarck. How often did the flags, including the blood flag of November 10th, have to be brought to safety by the police when they were informed that the Brame House was about to be stormed in a matter of minutes? Loyal men always took the banners from the flag hall to safe places beforehand. Only once did the police manage to capture the "harp sign of the movement."

On the first floor, the bronze bust of Dietrich Eckart, the deceased champion and friend of Adolf Hitler, greets visitors, serious and beautiful. In the middle, leading to the Senators' Hall, bronze plaques are set in on both sides. Large gold-plated laurel wreaths hang from them; they are the plaques that announce the names of those who fell on November 9th to posterity. Each time, before entering his workroom on the first floor, the Gübrer pauses for a moment in front of these tablets.

The small, modest casino is located in the basement. How often has the entire Brown House not sat together down here, along with A and party comrades from the movement and the Hitler Youth, listening to the loudspeakers that once again announced the election results and the election victories?

How often did the Gübrer sit in his patrol car and listen to the A-comrades, the Hitler boys and girls, tell him about their lives? The eyes of the men and boys did not shine! The eyes of the Führer's followers reflected the admiration for the beloved Führer, who had won such men and such youth for his cause!

On the ground floor are the rooms of the registry, the card library, the office, and the financial administration, where Master Odwarz exercised and still exercises his office with tenacious persistence. The first floor contains the rooms of the Führer, his adjutant and later deputy Heß, the adjutant Brückner, the rooms of the A, the political organization, and some offices for the Führer's office. The Propaganda Department is located on the second floor, followed by the A, the Legal Department, and the Prefecture Department, which later moved to the third floor. The A soon had its own house next to the "Braus." The archive and various technical offices are housed on the upper floors. Thus, the movement has its visible center.

Here, in this solid, sturdy house, the power of the movement is being symbolized. With this house, it shows all enemies, as well as the German people, the rise and strength that opponents trembled before. And the Munich post office will soon get used to properly delivering letters that only have the inscription: Brown House. This house is officially called Brienner Straße 45. Number 45 on Brienner Straße is the secret and soon-to-be public center of Germany. Millions of people look at this house. On the Obersalzberg, the Führer's great and bold ideas take form and plan; in the Brown House, they become flesh and blood.

Chief of Staff Victor Lube

From Adolf Hitler: My Struggle

People are not liberated by doing nothing, but through sacrifice.

The greatest right in this world is the right to the land that one wants to cultivate for oneself, and the greatest sacrifice is the blood that one sheds for this earth.

The religious teachings and institutions of a people must always be inviolable to the political leader; otherwise, he should not be a politician, but should become a reformer—if he has what it takes!

What was significantly Germanized in history was the land that our ancestors acquired with the sword and settled with German farmers.

The state does not represent an end, but a means. It is certainly the prerequisite for the formation of a higher human culture, but it is not the cause of it. Rather, this cause lies exclusively in the presence of a race capable of culture.

Anyone who loves their people only proves it through the sacrifices they are willing to make for them.

Since, for us, the state itself is only a form, while the essence is the nation—the people—it is clear that everything else must be subordinated to their sovereign interests.

The victory of an idea is all the more possible, the more comprehensively the propaganda has worked on the people as a whole and the more exclusive, streamlined, and solid the organization that carries out the struggle in practice.

The National Socialist worker must know that the prosperity of the national economy means his own material happiness. The National Socialist employer must know that the happiness and satisfaction of his employees is the prerequisite for the existence and development of his own economic greatness. National Socialist employees and employers are both representatives and stewards of the entire national community.

There is only reason to be proud of your people when you no longer need to be ashamed of your status. It must be a greater honor to be a citizen of this empire as a street sweeper than to be a king in a foreign state.

The German army is not there to be a school for the preservation of tribal peculiarities, but rather a school for mutual understanding and adaptation among all Germans.

As Marxism is being broken in Germany, its shackles are, in fact, breaking forever.

There was a new meeting at the Eberlbraukeller on October 1. 130 attendees came, and an attempt was made to blow up the Berjamunlung. This was carried out in the Crimea. A fortnight later, there was another rally with 170 attendees. The number of attendees began to rise rapidly. Soon, there were two hundred, then three hundred, people listening to the speaker, Adolf Hitler.

Unfortunately, in small circles, the NO DAP formed part of the German Workers' Party. The formulation of the 25 points began. This did not happen without fierce fighting, but in the end, the superior insight of the party's propaganda leader, Adolf Hitler, prevailed.

The Marxist press had already begun to address the new party. The first hateful articles appeared. Hitler's supporters began to speak in vivid terms. The movement was no longer unknown.

Although the speakers of the German Workers' Party were constantly insulted at foreign meetings, people still got to know them. Even the most stubborn Marxist had to recognize that there were other people besides Social Democrats and Communists, people who were not afraid of a clenched fist and were anything but bourgeois.

Within the party, the opponent was the Reidsleiter, Mr. Sharter, and Hitler. Harret felt that the approach Hitler was taking was too extreme, and when Hitler announced a call for a significant mass mobilization in the big hall of the Hofbräuhaus, Harret resigned from his post. He feared the collapse of the party. With all his energy, he challenged Hitler at the meeting, overcoming all concerns of public politicians with impetuosity.

Leaflets and posters were distributed. The style of the posters was a striking red, designed to stand out under any circumstances. Additionally, these red posters were particularly irritating to the Marxists, who believed they saw something offensive in the color. Hitler thought the most important task was to persuade the workers, whom he believed had been misled by Jewish leaders, to leave the left-wing movement. Before the rally took place, Hitler ensured that the party's program, which had taken a long time to complete, was available in print.

And then came that memorable February 24, 1920, the date of the party's official announcement, marked by the first significant battle of the movement and the cheers of 2,000 people celebrating the program.

Adolf Hitler

In honor of his valuable service, the State of Illinois

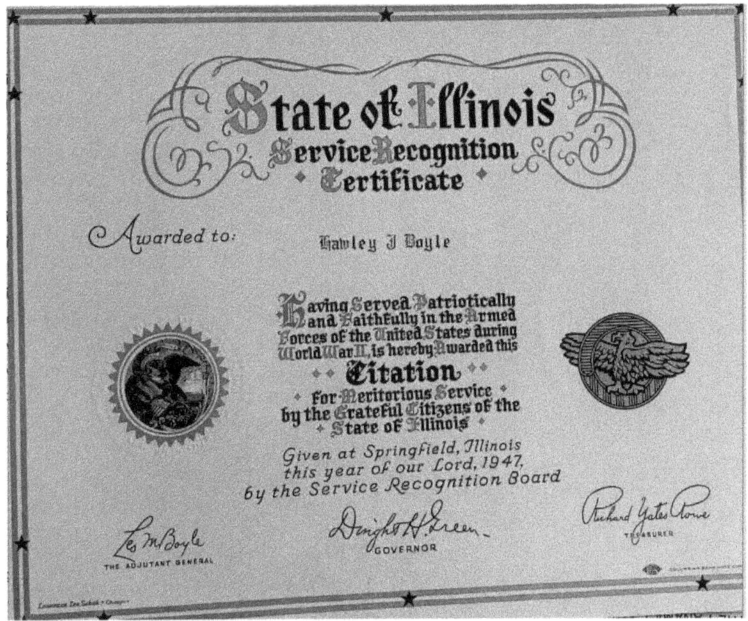

This collective literary work has been a lifelong journey taking fifty years to complete. Mitakuye Oaysin Honoring the unsung heroes that made this history lesson possible to be known. I'm proud to have known them and now know what they've done to teach history.

Adolf Hitler

Adolf Hitler was obsessed with the extermination of Native American Indians Trail of Tears.

Meetings and sometimes there were 4-5 in different cities in Germany, could take place on time in one day carried out.

The guide was often advised not to undertake this or that flight. But then his answer was always: If the necessity demands it, then I will fly even in a storm." How the opposing newspapers would have triumphed back then if the fixed flight plan had not been carried out or a proper meeting had been canceled. But Hitler helped them not the favor, and so one flight is particularly memorable, the Fürth- Frankfurt flight. The old Rohrbach, the first machine that the leader used at the time, was anchored with petrol panels. A storm hit the whole of Germany that was a rarity of this magnitude. There was a pan on take-off for general air traffic. Aur with difficulty.

Vith the D-2600 via Nuremberg. Arrival at the Nazi party rally in 1934.

Warrior • Victorious • Strong • Empowered • Survivor • Beautiful •
Alandra

Adolf Hitler

Vickie Boyle

A Native American Indian

Vickie Boyle &Jessica Diaz

Co- Author Jassica Diaz

110

Chapter 3

Kill the Indian to save the Man.

Association of Government Missions to Rule a Nation of Peoples, Adolf Hitler was obsessed with the Arian Nation. Inspired and implemented the Mission to the extermination of Jewish Peoples Jewish Holocaust.

The Elimination of Native Americans was a United States Government mission.

In 1879, Carlisle Boarding School was the first Boarding School with the Mission of killing the Indian to "Save" the man. Trail of Tears was implemented and Indians were removed to Reservations. Carlisle Boarding School opened in 1879 and operated for 30-plus years. Philosophy was for School Administrators to force the indigenous Indian children by removing them into White society.

They stripped them of their culture and religious beliefs. Cut their hair, warriors believed was spiritual strength not allowed to speak their language or talk about chiefs and Indian peoples.

Sioux Indians was a government name for people at Rosebud Reservation.

Daniel Milk - Carlisle Boarding School Sur-name. He was a Sioux Warrior at the age of 16 and was forced to leave St. Charles, South Dakota.

He entered the Boarding School on October 6, 1879, until July 6, 1885, from Rosebud Reservation. Stories of physical, sexual and permanent trauma were experienced by the Children. It's my honor to write about this family of survivors.

I'm humbled to show the association between the Jewish Holocaust and the American Indigenous Indians Removal Act Trail of Tears. Sgt. Hawley Boyle spoke of and saw the historical value of publishing this Book.

Daniel Milk Carlisle Boarding School member. Age, 16Rosebud Reservation Warrior.

Vickie Boyle &Jessica Diaz

Daniel Milk "Warrior"

The United States government declared, during the Indian Wars, against American Native Indians to Remove them from their Homeland. Stole their land and President Andrew Jackson destroyed any and everything associated with Native peoples. Their culture, languages, religions, songs way of life. Killed their main source of sustaining life with the American Bison, a main source of food, clothing, tools, and spiritual connection between the Native People and the Buffalo.

The mission to Relocate the Native Indian US Government soldiers forced them to leave what they knew of Home.

Notoriously known as Trail of Tears was implemented. The Genocide of thousands of Indian people died, mostly elderly and children.

To control the Indians that did make it to Reservations, President Andrew Jackson ordered the children to be taken from their parents and put in Boarding Schools, much like concentration camps during WWII, like Carlisle Boarding School that opened in 1879. Kill the Indian Save the Man's mission was to destroy the American Indian Race and turn the children into White Man's Civilization.

Daniel Milk was the Government's surname for him.

His Indian name was "Warrior." Age 16. He was one of the first students entered in the Carlisle School in 1879.

A Nez Perce boy was age 10 and a prisoner of War of the American Indian Wars. Nez Perce Indians, like the Lakota Sioux, refused to relocate during the Trail of Tears.

Students were restricted from speaking their Native language sing their Religions songs, they cut the boy's braided hair to strip them of their religious beliefs.

White priests and nuns abused the Indians, they lived in horrible conditions, Only favored children would get suits and dresses fit for Sunday School. Some were starved if they escaped or ran away. Eventually, the brainwashed Children believed they were Saved.

Vickie Boyle &Jessica Diaz

Carlisle Boarding School member

Daniel Milk / Warrior

Name: *Daniel Milk*

Indian name: *Warrior*

Tribe: *Sioux*   Age: *16*   Blood: *7.*

Agency: *Rosebud*

Father: *Milk*

Arrived: *10-6-79*   Departed: *7-6-85*   Cause: *[illegible]*

Class entered: Class left:

Trade: Outing:

Character:

Married: Deceased:

Remarks:

Add.- St. Charles, S.O. 1-21-73.

Adolf Hitler

Vickie Boyle

Chief Milk, father of Daniel Milk - Warrior. Daniel was among the first children taken from his parents and taken to Carlisle Boarding School.

Surviving family of the Carlisle Boarding School assimilation

Maevyn Stanley, the surviving heir of Daniel Milk-Warrior among the first students taken to Carlisle Boarding School. Maevyn lives with their stories of Carlisle Boarding School. When we met, a spiritual intervention of ancient ancestors put us together as we got acquainted and she braided my hair. I could feel the NDN spirit with each twist of the braid. She told me about her ancestors and I asked if I could have an interview with her. She kindly gave me this story of her ancestors. OSIYO GINALI Mitakuye Oaysin.

Adolf Hitler was obsessed with these types of Missions. The U.S. Government implemented the Indian, beginning with the Trail of Tears.

Mission orders: Worked in Station Hospital as a clerk in charge of 10 clerks in making up and issuing Hospital Publication.

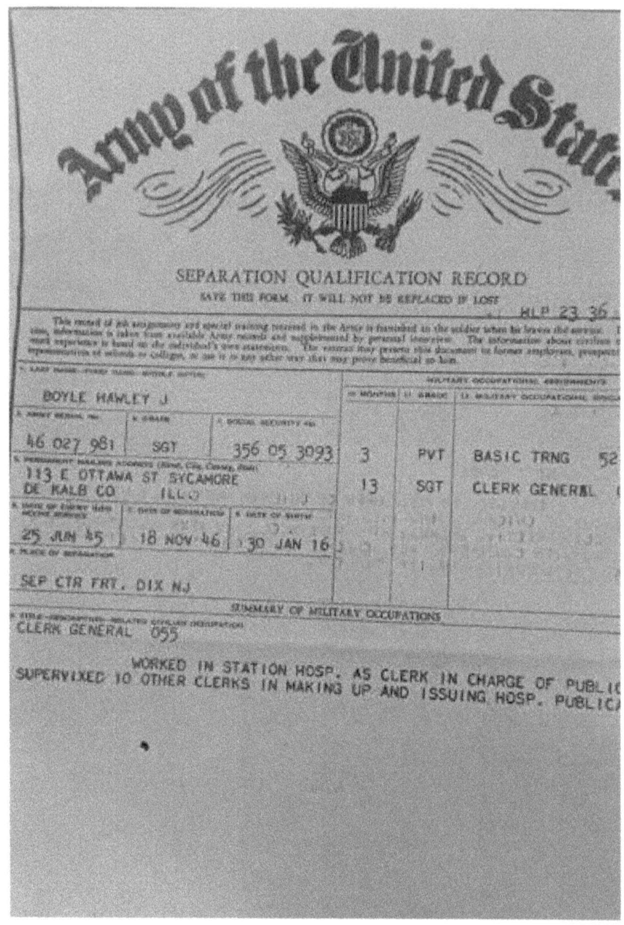

Honorable Discharge. Job well done, honoring your wishes that the German books would be translated from the German language to English.

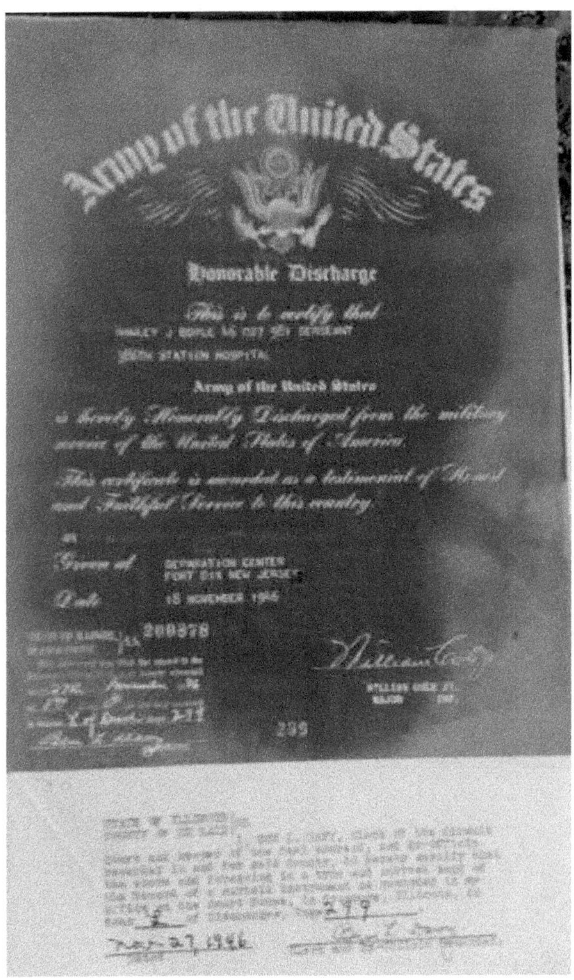

Vickie Boyle &Jessica Diaz

Kill the Indian

Save the Man.

White people's perspectives on treatment or events that were a cultural change were different than stories of abuse and torture told to Indian families.

One man's hatred for Native Indians decimated the Genocide of thousands of Native Indians.

We are still here, despite still being considered Prisoners of War. Life on Reservations continues to exploit their culture.

My honor to have an interview with "Warrior Milk's" great-great-granddaughter Maevyn Stanley, to bring this story of her family's historical trail of Horror.

The association of assimilation of a group of people who where American Native Indians and the US government's mission to eliminate their culture and languages and take their land.

Indian Hollcaust

Carlisle Boarding School student Warrior Milk Great great-granddaughter tells the family's story.

Casinos built on Indian Reservations will never repay the American Indians for their pain and suffering.

Adolf Hitler

As an proud American, some of our history needs to be retold so we may learn the lessons these Brave veterans and Indians have taught us.

Live in Peace, let no man's hatred become the Rule of Law.

Sgt. Hawley J Boyle

Sgt. Hawley J. Boyle became my father-in-law in the summer of 1975. He was witty, brilliant, tall, handsome, blue-eyed, a romantic poet, a Gentle Giant, a gentleman, and a scholar. He retired to Florida in 1970.

Hawley loved his granddaughter and always had a pack of M&M's in his shirt pocket for her, grinning ear to ear when she found them. Unfortunately, he didn't get to see his namesake grandson.

Hawley was an amazing, unsung hero of WWII, enlisting in the Army on June 25, 1945. He was assigned to the 386th Station Hospital, First Army, in Fort Dix, New Jersey.

He said he would have joined the Army sooner, but he was a civil firefighter in the Panama Canal and a newlywed. Like everyone else, he wanted to volunteer his military service to combat the genocide of Jews, better known as the Holocaust.

Hawley graduated from Lake Forest College in Chicago, Illinois. He earned tuition by working at the school, describing his job as the school bell ringer to begin each morning's classes. It was a huge bell and very heavy. It took his height and strength to pull the long rope to make it ring. He also helped clean the lunchroom, saying, "That's how I paid for my food. The food was really good too."

He was roommates with Richard Chamberlain. They were friends but had different interests: Richard studied acting, and Hawley was into sports. He lettered in four sports and was captain of the baseball team.

After he graduated, he played on a semi-pro team and became a sales agent for the Uniroyal Tire Company.

He took advantage of playing on the Constabulary Baseball Team during his tour in Germany and received a commendation letter from Commanding Colonel Edward J. Mahoney and General Harmon on September 2, 1946, congratulating him on winning the Constabulary Championship.

Hawley wrote love letters to his wife back home, talking about playing baseball. She had no clue about the atrocities he had seen, as he didn't want to upset her.

Sgt. Hawley Boyle, a Clerk General, was in charge of hospital publications. He supervised 10 other clerks issuing field hospitals' duties and publications. He had orders to destroy any Nazi propaganda, burning piles of Dr. Joseph Goebbels' publications in the street. He saw firsthand how the Nazi regime rose to power, fooled the German nation, and sought to eliminate the Jews and rule the world as a "super race."

Hawley smuggled a couple of books back to the United States out of the 13 volumes that Dr. Goebbels had distributed. These propaganda books were available in grocery stores to get the masses of Germans to purchase them. It was a political tactic to reach the German people.

Hawley witnessed the burning books in the streets and understood that it was part of the clever strategy to get the German people to elect Adolf Hitler into power as Chancellor of Germany.

We never read the manuscripts together—I wish we had. Because it was in Old German, we had to read between the lines and pictures. To my awe and amazement, 50 years later, I used Google Lens to translate the text of each page of these hardcover books with black-and-white pasted-in photographs.

This amazing account of the "War to End All Wars" is ending my life's literary work, ready for release.

In honor of Memorial Day,

Thank you to all who have served our great nation.

Honor Sgt. Hawley Boyle for his brave attempt to save historical books to teach about the horrific events of the Holocaust and the extermination of Jews by releasing these manuscripts.

My copyright lawyer found I was able to file a copyright © in its entirety for these books, "Mixed Messages," with the Library of Congress in May 1996, in order to teach the history of Adolf Hitler and the mixed messages of how he rose to power.

Hawley wanted to use these historical books to teach how the Holocaust happened, how it manifested, and to raise awareness of the minds that wanted to rule the world with a super race.

I hope he would approve of the books written in his honor and say we must learn that history does repeat itself.

Thank you for your service, Sir.

Sgt. Hawley J Boyle

About the Author

I'm retired living on the beautiful St. Johns River, promoting Anyresym Awareness saves Lives. I am so very Grateful Holy Father has given me the luxury to finish my life's literary work.

God Bless the United States of America. Once, an Indian Code Talker said to someone who asked why he joined the military during WWII. He said America is my Homeland and I will defend Her till my last breath.

Lululululululu ginali wado

www.ingramcontent.com/pod-product-compliance
Lightning Source LLC
Chambersburg PA
CBHW040146160726
48006CB00014B/1640